I0843688

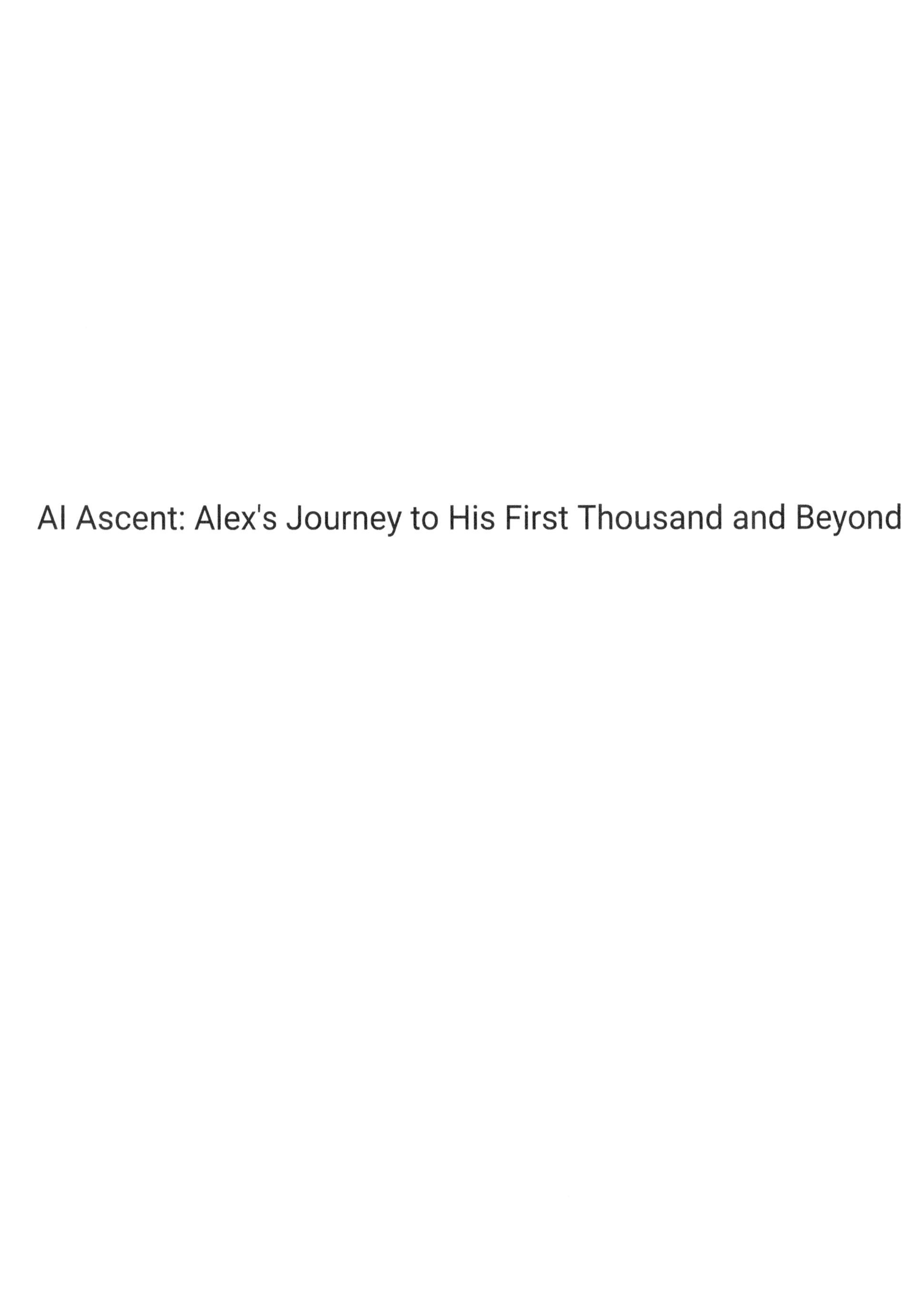

AI Ascent: Alex's Journey to His First Thousand and Beyond

Table of content

Chapter 1: Alex's First Brush with AI

 The sun had barely started its ascent when Alex's alarm blared. Unlike other days when he'd hit the snooze button multiple times, today was different. Today marked the beginning of his challenge, and his enthusiasm echoed the chirping birds outside.

Early Curiosity

As a child, Alex was no stranger to technology. From disassembling household gadgets to assembling Lego masterpieces, his hands were in perpetual motion. It was only fitting that during his high school years, he became enamored with the idea of robots. Not the kind from sci-fi movies, but the kind that could learn and evolve—AI. As he grew older, though, the enthusiasm was sidetracked by college coursework and the ensuing rush of life.

The challenge he faced now? A friendly bet from an old college mate, Sam, who teased, "With all your tech-talk, I bet you can't make a thousand bucks off this AI craze!" The wager was on.

Defining Artificial Intelligence

Alex began his quest the way he began any academic challenge: understanding the basics. He flipped open his laptop and typed, "What is Artificial Intelligence?" into the search bar.

The screen flooded with definitions, infographics, and video lectures. It was easy to feel overwhelmed, but Alex focused on the fundamental definition. At its core, AI involved creating algorithms that allowed computers to perform tasks that typically required human intelligence. This could range from recognizing patterns and images to making predictions based on vast amounts of data.

AI in Everyday Life

It didn't take long for Alex to realize that AI was already a part of his daily life. From the recommended movies on his streaming service to the voice assistant that updated him about the weather—these were all subtle implementations of AI. Even the traffic predictions on his daily commute app were guided by AI.

A Real-world Example

While understanding the foundational aspects, Alex stumbled upon a story about Sophia, a social humanoid robot developed by Hanson Robotics. Unlike any other robot, Sophia could display more than 50 facial expressions, engage in simple conversations, and even had Saudi Arabian citizenship. If machines could now hold citizenships, the world of AI was indeed vast and profound.

Mingling with AI Communities

To gain a deeper insight, Alex joined online forums and communities where AI enthusiasts, both beginners, and experts, discussed their projects, challenges, and successes. These platforms were gold mines of information, offering practical insights that no textbook could provide. The camaraderie in these forums was evident, and Alex felt right at home.

The Aha Moment

Late one evening, after hours of research, Alex experienced his first aha moment. While AI was complex, it wasn't inaccessible. With the right tools, resources, and determination, anyone could harness its power. And he was hell-bent on doing just that—not just for the thousand-dollar bet but to quench his renewed curiosity.

The stage was set. Alex was poised on the brink of an expedition into the AI realm, the stakes higher than ever before.

Chapter 2: Tackling the AI Learning Curve

Rediscovering the College Vibe

When was the last time Alex genuinely felt like a student? As he sat in his makeshift study, surrounded by scattered notes and open tabs delving deep into AI, memories of late-night college study sessions came flooding back. Back then, it was about grades and graduation. Now? It was personal.

Drowning in Information

AI was an ocean, vast and seemingly boundless. Alex could code, and he understood the basics of machine learning. However, the more he tried to pinpoint a starting point, the more overwhelmed he became. Neural networks, deep learning, natural language processing—where should he begin?

First Steps with Online Courses

Following advice from one of the online forums, Alex decided to kickstart his journey with structured online courses. He enrolled in a beginner's course on Coursera titled,

"Introduction to Artificial Intelligence." The structure of a syllabus, the weekly assignments, and peer discussions gave him a sense of direction.

The Struggles are Real

But it wasn't smooth sailing. Some concepts, especially in deep learning, were tricky. Alex would often find himself staring blankly at the screen, trying to wrap his head around algorithms and their workings. There were moments of doubt, too. Was he cut out for this? Could he genuinely make something out of AI?

Seeking Human Interaction

To complement his online learning, Alex began attending local AI workshops and seminars. Interacting with fellow AI enthusiasts face-to-face provided a fresh perspective. He could ask questions, witness live demonstrations, and understand the practical applications of what he was learning online. It was during one of these workshops that he met Lisa, a seasoned AI expert. Their conversations added layers to his understanding.

Eureka Moments

One evening, after a particularly grueling session trying to code a neural network, it clicked. The flow, the logic, the output—it all made sense. It was as if a mental block had been lifted. That night, Alex experienced the thrill that every creator, every innovator feels—the joy of creation and understanding.

Building a Small AI Project

With his newfound confidence, Alex decided to apply his knowledge. He started with a small project: an AI-powered chatbot for his personal blog. It was rudimentary, answering FAQs about him and his interests. But the satisfaction of seeing it interact with visitors? Priceless.

End of Chapter Thoughts

As Chapter 2 closes, we see Alex transition from an overwhelmed beginner to a budding AI enthusiast with a tangible project under his belt. The journey, peppered with ups and downs, teaches him persistence, the value of real-world interactions, and the unadulterated joy of creating something from scratch.

Chapter 3: The Freelance Awakening

New Horizons and Fresh Brews

Alex's mornings began to change. Instead of dreading the routine, he found himself eagerly booting up his computer, coffee in hand. His blog's chatbot was receiving surprisingly positive feedback, and it spurred a thought. Could he replicate such AI tasks for others and, perhaps, earn from it?

First Foray into Freelancing

Alex's best friend, Jamie, had often spoken about her freelance writing gigs. "You set your hours, pick your projects, and there's the joy of constant variety," she'd say. With a newfound realization of his potential in the AI realm, Alex decided to give freelancing a shot. He registered on platforms like Upwork and Fiverr, offering AI chatbot services.

A Humble Start

The beginning was predictably slow. As a newcomer, Alex had no reviews or a portfolio beyond his personal chatbot. Days turned into weeks with minimal traction. But instead of getting disheartened, he used this lull period to refine his skills further.

A Mentor's Guidance

Lisa, his acquaintance from the workshop, proved invaluable during this phase. Over shared cups of coffee, she shared her own experiences, emphasizing patience and persistence. "Market yourself," she advised. "Create samples, offer initial discounts, and most importantly, network."

The First Client

The notification was unexpected. A small e-commerce store wanted a chatbot for customer queries. Elated, Alex poured his heart and soul into the project. The outcome? A satisfied client, a five-star review, and a feeling of accomplishment.

Building Reputation

One project led to another. Word spread, and Alex's services began to gain traction. He expanded beyond chatbots, offering solutions like AI-powered recommendation systems for e-commerce and data analytics for small businesses.

Handling Challenges

Freelancing brought its own set of challenges. Deadlines, demanding clients, and occasional miscommunication tested Alex's patience and skills. But with each project, he not only improved his AI proficiency but also his client management tactics.

Broadening Horizons

With a steady stream of projects and an expanding portfolio, Alex pondered the next steps. Should he niche down, becoming an expert in a specific AI domain? Or should he diversify, exploring various AI facets? A conversation with Jamie gave him clarity. "Diversify first, understand where your passion truly lies, and then specialize," she suggested.

End of Chapter Reflection

Chapter 3 sees Alex's transition from a learner to a doer. He tastes the highs and lows of freelancing, realizing that technical prowess needs to be complemented with soft skills. As he stands at the crossroads of diversification and specialization, his journey becomes symbolic of many freelancers—finding their path in a vast world of possibilities.

Chapter 4: Discovering Niche AI Domains: The Goldmine Awaits

Deciphering the Buzzwords

With every new project and every online course, Alex came across terms and concepts that were previously alien to him. Generative Adversarial Networks (GANs), Sentiment Analysis, Computer Vision. As he delved deeper, it became evident: AI wasn't just one monolithic entity; it was a vast landscape with multiple niches.

The AI Conference that Changed Everything

It was a crisp autumn morning when Alex attended his first significant AI conference in the city. Everywhere he looked, there were booths showcasing AI applications from virtual fashion designing to predictive health analytics.

At one booth, he watched as a machine created art, translating simple sketches into detailed digital paintings. At another, he saw how AI could transform blurry videos into high-definition clips. The world of AI was so much grander than he'd imagined.

The Allure of Deepfake

One of the presentations at the conference was on the controversial domain of Deepfake technology. Alex watched in amazement as videos of celebrities saying things they'd never said played on the screen. The technology was impressive, but it also raised ethical concerns.

Finding His Passion: Natural Language Processing (NLP)

But it was a demonstration on NLP that truly captivated Alex. He saw how AI could understand, interpret, and generate human language. This wasn't just about chatbots; it was about creating tools that could write stories, analyze sentiments from massive data, or even assist in literary research. Alex felt a spark; he'd found his niche.

The Initial Dive into NLP

Eager to dive into this newfound interest, Alex began consuming everything NLP. He enrolled in specialized courses, participated in relevant forum discussions, and began experimenting with small NLP projects.

Practical Applications

His first major NLP task was for a local newspaper. They wanted a tool that could scan their archives and identify trends in public sentiment over the decades. It was a challenging project, but the outcome left the newspaper team in awe. They now had a tool that could provide insights into how public opinion had shifted over years, based solely on their article archives.

The Ethical Dilemmas

NLP, like all AI domains, had its ethical quandaries. Could a machine-written article replace human journalists? Should AI be used to generate literature? Alex grappled with these questions, realizing that with great power came immense responsibility.

Branching Out

His success with the newspaper project led to more clients seeking his NLP expertise. From analyzing customer reviews for businesses to assisting authors in understanding how readers might perceive their books, the applications seemed endless.

End of Chapter Thoughts

Chapter 4 paints a vivid picture of the expansive world of AI and the allure of specialized niches. As Alex immerses himself in NLP, readers witness the magic and challenges of making machines understand human language. Through his journey, the chapter highlights the confluence of technology, creativity, and ethics.

Chapter 5: AI Partnerships: Building Bridges with Fellow Enthusiasts

Coffee Conversations and New Ideas

One afternoon, as Alex sat in his favorite coffee shop working on an NLP project, he was approached by Maya, a young woman with a curious glint in her eyes. She had noticed Alex's work and introduced herself as a data scientist specializing in predictive analytics. Their casual conversation quickly morphed into an animated discussion about the potential of combining their skills.

The Genesis of a Joint Venture

Maya shared her vision of creating a tool that could predict market trends based on sentiment analysis of online news articles and social media posts. Alex was intrigued. Their combined expertise could make this a reality.

Pooling Resources

Both being freelancers, they were used to the solitary nature of their work. But the allure of collaboration was strong. They began meeting regularly, brainstorming and laying the groundwork for their tool. They rented a small workspace, pooling their resources to invest in more advanced AI hardware and software.

The Birth of 'TrendSage'

After months of development, 'TrendSage' was born—a tool that could predict market movements by analyzing vast amounts of textual data from the internet. Their initial tests were promising, with predictions often aligning with real-world market shifts.

Facing Skepticism

But not everyone was convinced. When they presented TrendSage at a tech startup event, many were skeptical of its accuracy and ethical implications. "Isn't this just another tool to manipulate markets?" one critic asked. Both Alex and Maya realized they needed to address these concerns head-on.

Ethics and Responsibility

They decided to introduce a transparency feature, showing users the data sources TrendSage used and the weightage given to each. They also incorporated feedback mechanisms, allowing users to report and rectify biases. This move was well-received, turning many skeptics into advocates.

Expanding the Team

With the increasing popularity of TrendSage, the duo recognized the need to expand. They hired a marketing expert, a UI/UX designer, and two more developers to refine the tool further and reach a broader audience.

Challenges of Partnership

While the collaborative venture was flourishing, it wasn't devoid of challenges. Differences in opinions, management styles, and visions often led to disagreements

between Alex and Maya. Yet, they found ways to communicate, compromise, and prioritize their shared goal over individual perspectives.

End of Chapter Reflection

Chapter 5 brings forth the power of collaboration in the world of AI. As Alex and Maya join forces, they not only amplify their technical prowess but also learn the nuances of teamwork, leadership, and managing a growing venture. Their journey is a testament to the idea that shared dreams, when pursued with respect and understanding, can lead to groundbreaking innovations.

Chapter 6: The Watershed Moment: TrendSage Goes Viral

From Unknown to Unmissable

Alex was accustomed to his usual routine — a balanced mix of work, learning, and leisure. But nothing could have prepared him for what was about to unfold. One morning, after releasing a predictive analysis on an upcoming tech product launch, TrendSage's predictions hit the bullseye, outperforming even the most seasoned industry analysts.

A Tweet That Started It All

Daniel Green, a renowned tech influencer with millions of followers, was the first to take notice. He tweeted: "Blown away by #TrendSage's spot-on prediction of the [Tech Product] sales. Are we witnessing a revolution in market analytics?". That tweet became the spark for a wildfire.

An Unanticipated Surge

Within hours, TrendSage was all over social media. The website traffic skyrocketed, leading to server crashes. Alex and Maya, caught off guard, scrambled to handle the massive influx. They urgently reached out to cloud service providers to scale up their infrastructure. While it was a chaotic day, it was also exhilarating. The world was watching, and they were at the center stage.

Media Spotlight

Major news outlets and tech magazines wanted to cover the story behind TrendSage. Invitations for interviews and podcasts poured in. Alex and Maya, once solitary freelancers, now found themselves navigating the maze of public relations, media management, and brand positioning.

Facing the Critics

With popularity came scrutiny. Many were amazed by TrendSage's capabilities, but others raised concerns. Questions about data privacy, the potential misuse of predictions, and the reliability of AI-driven insights were rampant. Alex and Maya knew they had to address these concerns head-on.

Holding a Public Webinar

In an era of skepticism, transparency was paramount. Alex and Maya decided to host a public webinar, explaining the workings of TrendSage, its data sources, the algorithms employed, and their approach to ethical AI. The webinar saw thousands of attendees, from curious students to industry veterans.

The duo tackled hard-hitting questions, addressing concerns while also highlighting the innovative aspects of their tool. By the end, many skeptics were converted, impressed by their dedication to openness and responsibility.

Building a Community

Realizing the power of community, Alex and Maya decided to launch a forum on their website, allowing users, enthusiasts, and critics to discuss, provide feedback, and share ideas about TrendSage. The forum rapidly became a vibrant space, fostering a sense of belonging and collective growth.

Preparing for the Future

The viral moment was a game-changer. Yet, it was clear that fleeting internet fame wouldn't sustain TrendSage. The tool had to evolve, improve, and continually adapt to remain relevant. With newfound resources, both financial and human, Alex and Maya started drafting a roadmap for the future. They aimed to make TrendSage not just a momentarily famous tool but an industry standard.

End of Chapter Reflection

Chapter 6 captures the whirlwind journey from obscurity to prominence. It underscores the unpredictable nature of success, the challenges of sudden fame, and the importance of grounded, ethical leadership. Through the lens of Alex and Maya, readers are taken on an exhilarating roller coaster, reminding them of the dual faces of virality — immense opportunities and daunting responsibilities.

Chapter 7: The Underbelly of Success: Facing Competition, Doubt, and Burnout

Emerging Competitors on the Horizon

The monumental success of TrendSage didn't go unnoticed. As months passed, several AI-driven market prediction tools started emerging. Some were blatant clones, while others touted unique features and improved algorithms. The market space, once dominated by TrendSage, now felt crowded.

The Allure of Venture Capital

With success came offers of significant investment. Venture capitalists saw potential in TrendSage and were eager to inject capital to scale it up even further. The sums of money being discussed were dizzying. But with large investments came the risk of losing creative control.

A Testing Partnership

Amidst this rapidly changing landscape, tensions between Alex and Maya began to surface. Maya, seeing the value in accepting venture capital, believed it could propel TrendSage to global dominance. Alex, on the other hand, was wary. He feared that external funding might dilute their original mission and make them slaves to investor demands.

The First Major Setback

A prominent business magazine published a feature comparing various market prediction tools. To Alex and Maya's dismay, TrendSage was ranked third. The critique pointed out areas of improvement, and while constructive, it felt like a blow. Doubt crept in. Had they peaked too soon? Were they being overtaken?

The Toll of Constant Hustle

While they grappled with external pressures, personal struggles weren't far behind. The long hours, constant media attention, and the weight of expectations began taking a toll. Alex started experiencing burnout. His passion for AI, once an insatiable fire, now felt like a smoldering ember.

Maya too faced challenges. She found herself constantly anxious, second-guessing decisions, and struggling with insomnia.

Seeking External Guidance

Recognizing that they couldn't navigate these waters alone, Alex and Maya decided to consult a business mentor. They approached Mrs. Lillian Hayes, a veteran in the tech industry with a reputation for turning around flagging startups.

Under Lillian's guidance, they began revisiting TrendSage's core values, identifying areas of genuine innovation, and understanding where they had gone astray.

Rekindling the Spark

Lillian emphasized the importance of self-care and mental well-being. She arranged for team-building retreats, workshops on stress management, and even introduced the team to mindfulness practices.

For Alex, it was a chance to reignite his love for AI. He began setting aside dedicated "innovation days" where he'd experiment without the pressures of business outcomes.

Maya, finding solace in mindfulness, started practicing meditation, grounding herself amidst the whirlwind of entrepreneurship.

End of Chapter Reflection

Chapter 7 delves deep into the challenges that often accompany rapid success. Through Alex and Maya's journey, the narrative highlights the personal and professional pitfalls that can emerge in the high-pressure world of startups. Their struggles serve as a poignant reminder that success is multifaceted, and maintaining it demands resilience, adaptability, and self-awareness.

Chapter 8: Rediscovery and Reinvention: The Renaissance of TrendSage

The Gentle Whispers of Doubt

As mornings turned into nights, Alex and Maya found themselves regularly reflecting on the essence of TrendSage. It was clear that to move forward, they needed to take a step back and remember why they started this journey in the first place.

Back to the Drawing Board

With Mrs. Lillian Hayes' encouragement, the duo decided to arrange a week-long offsite for the entire team. Nestled in a scenic mountain retreat, away from the hustle and bustle of city life, the goal was to rejuvenate and recalibrate.

Revisiting Old Ideas

During one of the brainstorming sessions, Alex stumbled upon his old notes from the initial days of TrendSage. The pages were filled with ideas that never made it to the final product—features that were sidelined in favor of other priorities.

Maya, too, had her "Aha!" moment when she unearthed customer feedback from TrendSage's beta version. She was reminded of features users had asked for, which got lost in the clamor of scaling up.

The Importance of User Feedback

One evening, the team decided to host a virtual townhall with some of TrendSage's earliest users. They listened intently as users shared their experiences, pointing out what they loved and areas where the tool could improve.

This session was an eye-opener. Alex and Maya realized they had been so focused on new customer acquisition that they'd somewhat neglected their core user base.

Pioneering Innovations

The offsite became a melting pot of ideas. The team came up with features that would set TrendSage apart from its competitors. They envisioned an 'AI Learning Hub', where users could understand the basics of AI, offering transparency and knowledge. They also conceptualized an 'Interactive Prediction Playground', allowing users to tweak parameters and see how different scenarios impacted predictions.

Rebranding and Marketing

Maya, harnessing her newfound energy, led the charge on rebranding. She believed that TrendSage needed a fresh look that reflected its evolution. Collaborating with graphic designers and branding experts, a more vibrant and dynamic brand identity was born.

Alex focused on outreach. He began engaging with AI communities, delivering webinars, writing articles, and showcasing the human side of TrendSage, emphasizing its roots and journey.

The Relaunch

After months of hard work, TrendSage 2.0 was ready. The relaunch event was a blend of tech demos, user testimonials, and personal anecdotes from Alex and Maya. The reception was overwhelmingly positive. TrendSage was not just back in the game; it was leading the charge.

End of Chapter Reflection

Chapter 8 underscores the magic that happens when founders reconnect with their original vision. By pausing, reflecting, and daring to reinvent, Alex and Maya set TrendSage on a path of sustained innovation and growth. This chapter is a testament to the idea that in the world of business, sometimes looking back provides the clearest vision for the future.

Chapter 9: Building Bridges: Embracing Collaborations and Partnerships

A Changing Landscape

In the tech ecosystem, no product or service exists in isolation. As TrendSage regained its foothold, Alex and Maya began recognizing the importance of collaborations and partnerships in fortifying their position in the market and reaching new frontiers.

Why Collaborate?

At a tech symposium in San Francisco, Alex attended a panel discussion on "The Power of Synergy in the AI Ecosystem." The insights from industry stalwarts resonated deeply. They emphasized that collaborations can lead to cross-pollination of ideas, sharing of resources, and opening up new customer bases. These thoughts planted the seed for TrendSage's collaborative journey.

Identifying Potential Partners

Maya spearheaded the initiative to identify potential collaborators. She looked into companies that complemented TrendSage rather than competed with it. The idea was to find organizations that shared their ethos, had a product or service that could integrate seamlessly with TrendSage, and had a mutual interest in exploring synergies.

The First Big Collaboration: DataStream Inc.

DataStream Inc., a data analytics firm specializing in real-time data streams from various industries, emerged as an ideal partner. Their vast data repositories could feed into TrendSage's algorithms, providing richer insights and more accurate predictions.

After a series of meetings, discussions, and brainstorming sessions, both teams realized the potential of their combined strengths. They decided to co-develop an enhanced version of TrendSage, integrating Data Streams real-time data feeds.

A Partnership with Academia

Alex always believed in the potential of fresh minds. He reached out to renowned universities, proposing a partnership where students could work on TrendSage for their projects, offering fresh perspectives and innovative solutions. The universities, seeing the value in offering hands-on experience to their students, were more than eager.

This partnership not only brought in a plethora of innovative ideas but also became a recruitment ground for TrendSage. The most promising students were offered internships and, eventually, full-time roles.

Global Expansions through Local Partners

To cater to global markets, understanding local nuances was essential. Instead of blindly venturing out, TrendSage collaborated with local partners in various regions. These partners, having a deep understanding of their respective markets, helped tailor TrendSage to fit local needs, ensuring its relevance and success across diverse geographies.

Challenges of Collaboration

Collaborations, while beneficial, weren't without challenges. Intellectual property rights, revenue sharing, and decision-making hierarchies needed careful negotiation. Maya, with her astute business acumen, often found herself mediating discussions, ensuring that collaborations remained mutually beneficial.

Nurturing Relationships

A significant part of successful collaborations was nurturing relationships. Regular check-ins, transparency in dealings, and joint celebrations of milestones played a vital role. Alex and Maya ensured that their partners felt valued and heard, turning business relationships into lasting friendships.

End of Chapter Reflection

Chapter 9 delves deep into the world of collaborations, highlighting their potential in amplifying growth and innovation. Through TrendSage's journey, readers are offered insights into the art and science of successful partnerships. The narrative emphasizes that in today's interconnected world, building bridges often leads to the most profound successes.

Chapter 10: Future Visions: Embracing Change and Pioneering New Frontiers

Gazing into the Horizon

With TrendSage firmly back on its trajectory of growth and innovation, Alex and Maya refused to rest on their laurels. They knew that in the rapidly evolving landscape of AI, complacency could be their undoing. It was time to look ahead, anticipate the future trends, and position TrendSage at the forefront of these revolutions.

Understanding the Quantum Leap

At a tech conference in Berlin, Alex stumbled upon a discussion on Quantum Computing. The potentials of this new realm of technology, capable of computations at unparalleled speeds, left him spellbound. The implications for AI were profound. Could TrendSage leverage this burgeoning technology?

Ethical Implications of AI

Maya, on the other hand, was increasingly concerned about the ethical implications of AI. She had witnessed firsthand the biases and prejudices that unchecked algorithms could perpetuate. There was a pressing need to ensure that TrendSage's predictions were not just accurate but also fair and unbiased.

The AI Ethics Board

Maya's concerns culminated in the formation of TrendSage's AI Ethics Board. Comprising external experts, sociologists, ethicists, and data scientists, the board was tasked with continuously reviewing TrendSage's algorithms, ensuring they adhered to the highest ethical standards.

Diving into Quantum AI

Back at TrendSage's headquarters, a dedicated Quantum AI team was formed. Partnering with leading quantum computing firms, the team embarked on the ambitious project of integrating quantum computations into TrendSage's predictions. The preliminary results were promising – predictions were faster, more accurate, and could process vast datasets like never before.

Sustainable AI: TrendSage's Green Initiative

Environmental concerns were becoming impossible to ignore. Reports highlighted the vast amounts of energy consumed by data centers powering AI algorithms. TrendSage, in its commitment to sustainability, embarked on a "Green AI" initiative. The goal was to optimize algorithms to be energy efficient and transition to renewable energy sources for their data centers.

Empowering the Next Generation

Education was a domain Alex and Maya were passionate about. They launched the "TrendSage AI Academy", offering courses on AI, data science, and quantum computing.

With a blend of online modules and hands-on workshops, the academy aimed to nurture the next generation of tech innovators.

Facing the Challenges Head-On

Every pioneering initiative brought its own set of challenges. The quantum realm was uncharted territory, with its own set of complexities. Ethical considerations often clashed with business objectives, requiring delicate balancing. The green initiative demanded significant investments. Yet, with each challenge, Alex and Maya's resolve only strengthened.

Future-Proofing TrendSage

With the multitude of initiatives, TrendSage was not just adapting to the future; it was shaping it. Regular "FutureScape" workshops became a fixture, where the team envisioned the next five, ten, and twenty years, ensuring TrendSage remained not just relevant but pioneering in its endeavors.

End of Chapter Reflection

Chapter 10 offers a deep dive into the futuristic vision of TrendSage. From quantum leaps to ethical considerations and environmental responsibilities, it paints a picture of a company that is not just reactive but proactive in its approach. Through Alex and Maya's journey, readers are reminded of the importance of foresight, adaptability, and a steadfast commitment to values in the face of rapid technological advancements

Chapter 11: The Human Touch: Marrying AI with Emotional Intelligence

The Digital Paradox

As TrendSage's algorithms became more sophisticated and its predictions more precise, a new challenge surfaced. Users began expressing that while the tool was unparalleled in its capabilities, it felt somewhat "cold" and "impersonal." This revelation led Alex and Maya to delve into the realms of Emotional Intelligence (EI) and its integration with AI.

Why Emotional Intelligence Matters

One evening, over cups of steaming coffee, Maya shared an anecdote about a consultation she had with a local business owner. He expressed that while TrendSage gave him great insights, he missed the "gut feeling" he got from human interactions. This led to an enlightening conversation about the importance of human emotions, intuitions, and relationships in decision-making.

Exploring the Intersection of AI and EI

The duo decided to explore how they could make TrendSage not just smart, but also emotionally intuitive. They began by hiring experts in the field of psychology, neuroscience, and human-computer interaction.

EmoTech: The New Division

A new division, named "EmoTech," was formed. Their mission was to weave emotional intelligence into the very fabric of TrendSage. They aimed to ensure that while users interacted with the platform, they felt understood, valued, and emotionally connected.

The Empathy Algorithm

One of EmoTech's pioneering innovations was the "Empathy Algorithm." This tool gauges user emotions based on their interactions with TrendSage. If a user seemed frustrated, the system would respond with supportive messages or offer to simplify processes. If a user achieved a significant milestone using the platform, TrendSage would celebrate with them, offering congratulatory messages and animations.

Understanding Cultural Nuances

Alex and Maya were well aware that emotions and their expressions vary widely across cultures. Collaborating with anthropologists and cultural experts, EmoTech began the herculean task of understanding and incorporating cultural nuances into TrendSage's emotional responses.

Personalized User Experiences

Building upon the Empathy Algorithm, the system began to offer personalized experiences. Users could now customize the look, feel, and interactions based on their preferences. Whether it was a calming blue interface for someone seeking tranquility or an energetic red for those needing motivation, TrendSage adapted seamlessly.

Challenges and Ethical Considerations

While the integration of EI into AI was groundbreaking, it wasn't without challenges. Privacy concerns arose, with users feeling apprehensive about a machine "reading" their emotions. Maya, with her unwavering commitment to ethics, ensured transparency in how emotional data was used and stored.

The Resounding Success

The introduction of EI into TrendSage was met with overwhelming acclaim. Users expressed that the platform now felt more like a supportive partner than just a tool. This human touch, combined with TrendSage's unmatched analytical capabilities, solidified its position as an industry leader.

End of Chapter Reflection

Chapter 11 delves into the intricacies of blending technology with humanity. It underscores the importance of understanding and catering to the emotional needs of users, even in a domain as analytical as AI. Through Alex and Maya's journey, readers are reminded that at the heart of every technological endeavor, the end goal is to enhance human experiences.

Chapter 12: Bridging the Gap

Democratising AI for Small Businesses

The Forgotten Backbone

Alex and Maya had been so engrossed in developing TrendSage and ensuring its scalability for large corporations that they had overlooked a crucial segment – small businesses. On a trip to a local market, Alex was inspired by the tenacity of small business owners and their ability to adapt despite limited resources. It made him wonder: Could TrendSage be the resource they were missing?

Unlocking Potential with Affordable Solutions

The reality hit hard. Most small businesses couldn't afford the premium packages of TrendSage. This realization sparked a new mission for Alex and Maya – to democratize AI for small businesses, enabling them to harness its power without burning a hole in their pockets.

Understanding the Needs

Maya initiated a series of focus group discussions with local business owners. From bakers to crafters, each had a unique perspective and a set of requirements. While some sought insights on customer preferences, others wanted assistance in inventory management.

TrendSage Lite: The Revolution

The feedback was crystal clear. Small businesses needed something straightforward, intuitive, and cost-effective. The answer was "TrendSage Lite" – a simplified, affordable version of TrendSage tailored to meet the specific needs of small businesses.

Feature Customization

Realizing that a one-size-fits-all approach wouldn't work, TrendSage Lite allowed businesses to pick and choose features relevant to them. A local cafe might opt for insights on popular menu items and peak business hours, while a crafts store might prefer trend predictions and supply chain management.

Empowering Through Education

Alex believed that just offering a tool wasn't enough. These business owners, many of whom weren't tech-savvy, needed to understand how to leverage AI effectively. TrendSage AI Academy expanded its curriculum to offer courses and workshops specifically for small business owners, ensuring they had the knowledge to make the most of TrendSage Lite.

Local Heroes: Community Integration

In a heartwarming initiative, TrendSage partnered with local communities. Every month, TrendSage Lite showcased a "Local Hero" – a small business that had innovatively utilized AI to boost their operations. This not only offered them exposure but also inspired other businesses to experiment and innovate.

Facing Skepticism

Change is often met with resistance. Many small business owners were skeptical about integrating AI into their operations, fearing it might replace the human touch that defined them. Through workshops, demos, and success stories, Alex and Maya worked tirelessly to dispel these myths, showcasing how AI could be a tool of empowerment rather than replacement.

The Blossoming Impact

As months turned into years, the impact of TrendSage Lite was palpable. Small businesses that had previously struggled were now thriving. They had insights at their fingertips, predictive analyses guiding their strategies, and the power of AI bolstering their growth.

End of Chapter Reflection

Chapter 12 serves as an inspiring testament to the power of inclusivity. Through Alex and Maya's journey, readers witness the transformative power of technology when it's made accessible to all, regardless of scale or financial capabilities. The narrative reaffirms the belief that innovation, when shared generously, can uplift entire communities.

Chapter 13: Beyond Business: Using AI to Make a Social Impact

A Revelation in the Rainforest

The adventure began unexpectedly. On a trip to the Amazon Rainforest, Maya was astounded by the intricate balance of nature. Yet, she also saw the scars of deforestation and the adverse impacts of climate change. As she spoke with local communities, she realized the gravity of the challenges they faced. Maya wondered: Could TrendSage play a role in addressing some of these issues?

A Calling Beyond Profits

Returning to the headquarters, Maya shared her experiences with Alex. Together, they decided that TrendSage had a responsibility beyond business. The duo began brainstorming on ways AI could contribute positively to environmental and social causes.

Project GreenSight

The first initiative was "Project GreenSight." Using AI, TrendSage began analyzing deforestation patterns, predicting vulnerable zones, and aiding conservationists in strategizing protective measures. These insights also proved instrumental in lobbying for stricter forest protection regulations.

CleanWave: Tackling Ocean Pollution

Ocean pollution, particularly plastic waste, had become a monumental challenge. TrendSage's next venture, "CleanWave," employed AI-powered drones to identify and map high-density plastic waste regions in oceans. Collaborating with cleanup crews, these areas were targeted for waste removal and recycling.

AidSage: Humanitarian Assistance

Natural disasters often struck with little warning, leaving communities devastated. "AidSage" was TrendSage's answer to this. By analyzing weather patterns, geographical data, and historical trends, AidSage predicted potential disaster zones, allowing NGOs and government bodies to pre-position resources and devise evacuation plans.

Socio-Econ AI: Boosting Rural Economies

In collaboration with economists and social scientists, TrendSage developed "Socio-Econ AI." This platform assisted rural communities in identifying sustainable economic opportunities based on their local resources, culture, and strengths, ensuring they had avenues for growth without compromising their heritage.

The Ethical Quandary

While these initiatives were groundbreaking, they weren't devoid of challenges. Balancing data privacy with humanitarian goals was a tightrope walk. Maya and Alex ensured that every project adhered to strict ethical standards, keeping community consent and well-being at the forefront.

Collaborations and Partnerships

Understanding the vast scope of these projects, TrendSage began forming alliances with global NGOs, environmental organizations, and governments. These collaborations not only provided on-ground expertise but also ensured the solutions were holistic and well-integrated.

Global Recognition and Expansion

The impact of TrendSage's social initiatives was undeniable. Recognized globally, the company received numerous accolades. But for Alex and Maya, the true reward was witnessing tangible positive change in the communities and environments they had touched.

End of Chapter Reflection

Chapter 13 delves deep into the transformative power of technology when directed towards societal and environmental good. Through TrendSage's journey, readers witness the seamless melding of business acumen with a humanitarian spirit. It serves as a beacon, highlighting the possibilities that emerge when technology is used as a force for good.

Chapter 14: Embracing Diversity: Building a Global AI Ecosystem

The Seed of an Idea

One evening, as Alex was tuning into a global tech summit, he was captivated by the diverse array of speakers from various corners of the world, each bringing unique perspectives on AI. This was the seed of a thought: to truly make TrendSage universal, they needed to embrace this global diversity.

A Symphony of Cultures

In their pursuit of refining TrendSage, Alex and Maya had primarily focused on western markets. They realized the potential of incorporating insights from diverse cultures, traditions, and socioeconomic backgrounds to enrich their AI platform.

The Global Outreach Program

To bring this idea to life, they launched the "Global Outreach Program." Its objective was to collaborate with tech enthusiasts, local businesses, and communities from different countries and understand their unique challenges and aspirations.

Collaborating with Africa

One of their first collaborations was in Africa. Partnering with tech startups in Nairobi, they unearthed how AI could support agriculture, predicting weather patterns and analyzing soil health to aid farmers.

The Asian Resonance

In Asia, with its mosaic of cultures and a booming tech industry, TrendSage collaborated with local enterprises in India, South Korea, and Thailand. They explored everything from urban planning in densely populated cities to leveraging AI in traditional crafts, ensuring that technology respected and uplifted cultural nuances.

Latin American Rhythms

Latin America, with its rich history and vibrant cultures, offered insights into areas like sustainable tourism, indigenous knowledge systems, and local crafts. By integrating these insights, TrendSage became a tool that resonated deeply with local businesses and artisans.

Challenges of Global Integration

While the vision was grand, the path was fraught with challenges. Language barriers, differing technological infrastructures, and diverse regulatory landscapes made the process complex. Yet, Alex and Maya were undeterred. They built a multicultural team, with experts proficient in various languages and familiar with regional nuances.

A Platform that Speaks Your Language

One of the groundbreaking features introduced was a multilingual interface, allowing users to interact with TrendSage in their native tongue. This wasn't just about translating words but also adapting content to be culturally relevant.

The Global AI Conference

To celebrate this journey and foster further collaborations, TrendSage initiated the annual "Global AI Conference." This event brought together thought leaders, innovators, and communities from across the world, fostering a space for shared learning and mutual growth.

End of Chapter Reflection

Chapter 14 chronicles the exhilarating journey of TrendSage as it weaves into the fabric of global communities. It emphasizes the value of diverse thought, the richness of varied experiences, and the potential of a collaborative spirit.

Chapter 15: The Ethical Frontier: Navigating AI's Moral Compass

The Unintended Ripple

It started with a seemingly benign update to TrendSage. Within days, user feedback began to flood in. Some users were thrilled, but a fraction felt that the AI's recommendations were biased, perpetuating certain stereotypes. Alex and Maya were confronted with a critical question: Had they inadvertently let biases seep into their AI?

Bias in Code

Upon investigation, they discovered that certain datasets used to train TrendSage had subtle biases. These biases reflected societal prejudices, which, when magnified by AI, had far-reaching implications. It was a stark reminder: AI isn't immune to human flaws.

An Ethical Epiphany

This incident became a turning point. Alex and Maya realized that they needed to prioritize ethical considerations as much as technical advancements. AI ethics wasn't just about avoiding biases; it encompassed data privacy, user consent, transparency, and accountability.

Assembling the Ethical Task Force

To address these concerns, they formed an "Ethical Task Force" comprising of technologists, ethicists, sociologists, and community representatives. This diverse group was tasked with evaluating TrendSage's ethical framework and ensuring its adherence to the highest moral standards.

Transparency by Design

One of the task force's initial endeavors was to make TrendSage's algorithms more transparent. While proprietary elements remained protected, users were given insights into how decisions were made and how data was processed.

Bias-Busting Initiatives

To tackle the bias challenge head-on, the team initiated a series of "Bias-Busting Workshops." These aimed to educate developers on recognizing and countering biases. Further, they integrated bias-detection tools within TrendSage, ensuring that the AI constantly self-evaluated and corrected skewed patterns.

A User-Centric Approach

Recognizing that AI's power shouldn't overshadow user autonomy, new features were introduced. Users could now set ethical boundaries for the AI, ensuring it operated within their comfort zones. This democratized control, ensuring that AI was a tool for users, not a force upon them.

Global Ethical Collaborations

Alex and Maya realized that AI ethics was a global concern. They reached out to other tech giants and academic institutions, leading to the formation of the "Global AI Ethics

Consortium." This body worked on establishing universal ethical guidelines for AI development and deployment.

Rebuilding Trust

While the journey to ethical optimization was challenging, it was also rewarding. Over time, as users noticed TrendSage's commitment to ethical transparency, their trust in the platform was restored and even strengthened.

End of Chapter Reflection

Chapter 15 delves deep into the heart of AI's moral challenges, illustrating that technology's soul is as crucial as its code. Through Alex and Maya's trials, readers are prompted to reflect on the balance between innovation and integrity.

Chapter 16: Rise of the Machines? Debunking AI Myths

A Hollywood Moment

It was during a casual movie night that Alex and Maya watched a sci-fi film depicting AI-driven machines turning against humanity. As the credits rolled, Alex chuckled, "Isn't it interesting how popular culture often paints AI as this ominous force?" Maya nodded, realizing that many held fears and misconceptions about AI due to such portrayals.

The Myth Landscape

As leaders in the AI domain, they knew many myths surrounded this transformative technology. Some believed AI could spontaneously gain consciousness, while others saw it as an imminent job-stealer. There were concerns about AI's potential misuse and the belief that it was an infallible force.

Myth-Busting Campaign

To address these misconceptions, TrendSage embarked on a "Myth-Busting Campaign." Its mission? To demystify AI, educate the masses, and lay down factual foundations.

Myth 1: AI Can Think and Feel

Contrary to popular belief, AI doesn't "think" or "feel" like humans. It processes data and follows predefined algorithms. Alex and Maya emphasized that while AI can simulate understanding or emotions, it doesn't possess consciousness.

Myth 2: AI Will Replace All Jobs

While AI can automate specific tasks, it cannot replicate human creativity, empathy, or complex problem-solving entirely. Many jobs would evolve, and new roles would emerge in an AI-driven world. The duo highlighted the idea of working alongside AI, harnessing its capabilities while capitalizing on human strengths.

Myth 3: AI is Unerring

The belief that AI is infallible was addressed head-on. Alex and Maya demonstrated instances where TrendSage made errors or needed adjustments. AI is as good (or flawed) as the data it's trained on.

Interactive Workshops and Webinars

To reach a broader audience, TrendSage organized workshops, webinars, and interactive sessions in schools, colleges, and community centers. These sessions allowed attendees to interact with AI tools directly, dispelling fears and fostering understanding.

AI for Kids

One standout initiative was "AI for Kids." Through interactive storytelling and hands-on projects, children learned about AI's basics. This early exposure ensured that the next generation grew up informed and open-minded about AI's possibilities.

Collaborative Public Art Installations

In a creative twist, TrendSage collaborated with artists to create public art installations demystifying AI. These interactive pieces combined technology and art, allowing visitors to engage with AI in unexpected, enlightening ways.

End of Chapter Reflection

Chapter 16 takes readers on a journey to separate AI fact from fiction. Through Alex and Maya's dedicated initiatives, we see the importance of education, transparency, and open dialogue in shaping a balanced perspective on emerging technologies.

Chapter 17: Uncharted Waters: Exploring New Frontiers with AI

The World Beyond the Obvious

In the ever-evolving landscape of technology, resting on one's laurels is the quickest path to obsolescence. As TrendSage continued to flourish, Alex and Maya felt an insatiable urge to push boundaries further. What if AI could be applied in areas previously unthought of?

Deep Sea and AI

The deep-sea, largely unexplored and mysterious, caught their attention. Collaborating with marine biologists, they wondered if TrendSage could assist in understanding oceanic patterns, marine life behaviors, and the mysteries of the underwater world.

AI in Space

But why stop at Earth? The vast expanse of space beckoned. Teaming up with astronomers and space agencies, they began experiments to see if TrendSage could predict cosmic events, analyze extraterrestrial data, or even assist in the search for other habitable planets.

Unearthing History

Back on terra firma, history provided fertile ground. Archaeologists were intrigued by the possibility of AI detecting patterns or anomalies in ancient artifacts, potentially offering insights into long-lost civilizations. Could AI, Alex and Maya pondered, be the modern-day Rosetta Stone?

The Healing Touch

Medicine, with its intricate complexities, posed another challenge. While AI had made inroads into diagnostics, the duo dreamt bigger. What if TrendSage could aid in understanding mental health patterns, making therapy more accessible and tailored?

Sonic Resonance

Music, the universal language, wasn't left out. In partnership with musicians and sound therapists, experiments were launched to see if AI could generate therapeutic soundscapes, aiding in meditation, relaxation, and healing.

Environmental Guardians

Climate change, the pressing concern of the age, beckoned. Environmentalists and TrendSage developers came together, brainstorming on AI-driven solutions for pollution control, biodiversity conservation, and predicting natural calamities.

Trials, Triumphs, and Turbulence

Not all ventures were smooth sailing. While AI's foray into deep-sea exploration unveiled stunning bioluminescent wonders, space explorations faced data overloads. History projects were fruitful, offering clues into ancient trade routes, but medical initiatives raised ethical concerns that needed careful navigation.

End of Chapter Reflection

Chapter 17 showcases the audacious spirit of innovation. By venturing into uncharted domains, Alex and Maya not only expand TrendSage's horizons but also prompt readers to dream beyond conventional boundaries.

Chapter 18: Embracing Global Collaborations: The AI Renaissance

The Dream Beyond Borders

The vision that had started in a humble dorm room was now making waves globally. TrendSage had become a beacon in the AI community, but Alex and Maya were far from done. They believed that to truly harness AI's potential, global collaboration was essential. Different cultures, perspectives, and expertise could spark a renaissance in AI development.

The Inception of AI Connect

With this idea, AI Connect was born. An international convention dedicated to bridging AI innovators from every corner of the world. Hosted in a different country each year, it became the melting pot of ideas, fostering collaboration and cross-pollination of concepts.

The Swiss Collaboration: AI and Time

In Switzerland, they met Dr. Lena Weber, a pioneer in temporal algorithms. Together, they explored how AI could predict market trends based on historical data, not just from a financial perspective, but socio-cultural trends too.

Nigeria's AI-driven Agritech

From Africa, Alex and Maya were introduced to innovative agritech solutions. Using AI-driven drones, local farmers could predict weather patterns, optimize irrigation, and improve crop yields. Collaborating with Nigerian tech entrepreneurs, TrendSage integrated these solutions, giving small-scale farmers access to world-class technology.

AI Harmonies in Japan

In the Land of the Rising Sun, they collaborated with maestros who were intertwining AI with traditional Japanese music. TrendSage began facilitating the creation of music that beautifully blended the old with the new, producing harmonies that resonated across generations.

Brazil's Green Tech Evolution

Brazil's lush rainforests became the backdrop for an eco-venture. Partnering with environmentalists in the Amazon, they developed AI tools that could monitor deforestation in real-time, empowering local tribes and governments to protect their sacred lands more effectively.

The Universal AI Language

A standout project was the development of an AI-driven universal translation tool. With contributors from across the globe, the tool was designed to break down language barriers, fostering clearer communication and understanding in real-time.

Challenges of Global Synergy

But global collaborations weren't without their challenges. Navigating regulatory hurdles, understanding cultural nuances, and managing time zones required finesse. Yet, every challenge faced only strengthened their resolve and enriched their learning.

End of Chapter Reflection

Chapter 18 encapsulates the power of collective intelligence. As Alex and Maya traverse the globe, their journey highlights that the true essence of AI lies in its ability to unify, transcend boundaries, and catalyze a brighter, interconnected future.

Chapter 19: Ethical Quandaries: Navigating the Moral Maze of AI

Awakening to Ethical Implications

Success always brings new challenges. As TrendSage expanded, and AI found its footing in various sectors, unforeseen ethical concerns emerged. News of AI mishaps – from biased algorithms to privacy breaches – began making headlines, and the public started asking hard-hitting questions.

The Bias Conundrum

One afternoon, a journalist cornered Alex at a tech conference. "Is it true that TrendSage's recruitment tool showed gender bias?" The question stung. Upon investigation, Alex and Maya discovered that the AI had unintentionally favored male resumes due to inherent biases in the training data. They realized that if left unchecked, AI could perpetuate societal biases.

Privacy Paradox

Then there was the issue of data privacy. As TrendSage's applications delved deeper into user preferences to offer personalized experiences, concerns about data misuse and surveillance grew. Maya received emails from worried users questioning the depth of data TrendSage accessed.

Autonomy vs. Control

The medical applications of TrendSage posed another dilemma. If AI recommended a particular treatment, who bore the responsibility for its consequences? The doctor? The patient? The developers?

Stepping Up: Ethical AI

Realizing the weight of these issues, Alex and Maya launched an "Ethical AI" initiative within TrendSage.

Bias Auditing: Regular audits were conducted on algorithms to identify and rectify biases. They also organized workshops to educate developers about ethical coding.

Transparent Policies: Clear data handling and privacy policies were established, ensuring users knew exactly how their data was utilized.

Collaborative Decision-making: In sectors like medicine, TrendSage's AI was repositioned as an advisory tool, ensuring that the final decision rested with humans.

Ethics Committee: An independent committee, comprising philosophers, tech experts, and sociologists, was established to scrutinize and guide the ethical dimensions of TrendSage's projects.

Global Ethical AI Symposium

To address the industry-wide implications, TrendSage, under Alex and Maya's guidance, hosted the first-ever Global Ethical AI Symposium. Here, tech giants, startups, policymakers, and ethicists came together to draft a universal ethical framework for AI development and deployment.

End of Chapter Reflection

Chapter 19 delves deep into the murky waters of AI ethics, underscoring the importance of moral responsibility in tech advancements. Through Alex and Maya's proactive approach, readers learn that while technology can be neutral, its applications seldom are.

Chapter 20: A New Dawn: Envisioning an AI-Integrated Future

The Winds of Change

As years rolled on, AI, once a niche concept, became an inextricable part of everyday life. Homes, workplaces, transport systems, and even leisure activities bore the unmistakable imprint of AI's influence. The world stood at the cusp of a new era, and at the forefront of this revolution were Alex, Maya, and TrendSage.

The Age of Augmented Humanity

Instead of being feared as a replacement for humans, AI began to be seen as a tool for augmentation. Surgeons used AI to make more precise incisions; teachers used it to create customized learning plans; artists collaborated with AI to craft masterpieces that were beyond human imagination alone.

AI for All

TrendSage launched a series of community programs titled "AI for All." These initiatives aimed to democratize AI access, ensuring even the remotest parts of the world could benefit from its wonders. From AI-driven farming techniques in rural Africa to language-learning tools in remote Asian hamlets, the vision of inclusive growth took shape.

The Next Generation

Alex and Maya, once young college students with a dream, were now global tech leaders. But they never forgot their roots. They established scholarships, internships, and training camps, nurturing the next generation of AI enthusiasts.

Reflections and Revelations

One evening, at the TrendSage headquarters' rooftop, overlooking a bustling city illuminated with digital wonders, Alex mused, "Did we ever imagine we'd come this far?" Maya, with a gleam in her eye, replied, "We didn't just imagine, we built it."

But with all their accomplishments, they acknowledged the journey wasn't theirs alone. It was a testament to human ingenuity, collaboration, resilience, and the unyielding spirit to push boundaries.

The Horizon Beyond

The duo had another dream – to make AI not just a tool but a companion. They envisioned a future where AI understood human emotions, aspirations, and dreams, guiding them not based on data alone but also on empathy and understanding.

End of Chapter Reflection

Chapter 20 encapsulates the transformative journey of AI, from being a disruptive technology to an integral part of human existence. Through Alex and Maya's eyes, readers witness the awe-inspiring potential of harmonizing technology with human spirit and values.